UK AIRPORTS

AUSTIN J. BROWN

IAN ALLAN
Publishing

To Annetta and Nico

UK AIRPORTS

First published 1993

ISBN 0 7110 2139 2

© Austin J. Brown 1993

Published by Ian Allan Ltd, Shepperton, Surrey; and printed by Ian Allan Printing Ltd at its works at Coombelands in Runnymede, England.

Front cover:
Aberdeen's distinctive control tower shelters a Lakeside Titan from a passing thunderstorm, illuminated by the strong October sun.

Back cover:
The South African Airways Boeing 747SP ZS-SPE is manoeuvred through the gates and across the perimeter road outside the British Airways maintenance base at Heathrow in May 1989.

Title page:
Flight One's Twin Pioneer, highlighted by the low autumn sun while parked by the new control tower complex at Gloucestershire Airport.

ACKNOWLEDGEMENTS

The publishers and I would like to offer our grateful thanks to all of the Airport Directors and their Press and Public Relations Officers who allowed us to work airside, and to their staff who escorted us, as the law now requires. The waiving of landing fees and the helpful assistance of air traffic controllers kept our account in the black and made the whole job so much more pleasant. I am sure this shows in the photographs. To Shari Peyami, Chris Huxtable and the whole crew at Wycombe Air Centre for their enthusiasm and operational support of the Cessna 172 we borrowed from them, to David and Claire Morris of Top Farm for the Cessna 150, Keith Whyham of ANT at Blackpool who helped us after our fire extinguisher discharged, Julian and Sue Roach at Welshpool, Sue Boxall at Newcastle Aero Club who brought one of our magnetos back to life, Ian and Angela MacFarlane, also at Newcastle, and Biffo and Gill Bannister, who helped us in Leeds. Last but by no means least, Dick Flute, who flew three-quarters of the route, and is the only pilot I know who literally cannot get lost in the UK when flying VFR as he has driven over it comprehensively with an HGV for the last twenty-five years, and is a very observant character! Dick has written the story of our trip which is also published by Ian Allan as From the Flightdeck: Cessna 172 Round Britain.

CONTENTS

INTRODUCTION

Ian Allan Publishing came to me in 1992 and asked me to produce a pictorial essay on activities at Britain's airports. It did not take very many minutes to realise that most of the material in my extensive library was obsolete, either by virtue of recent airport development, even during this recession, or by changing airlines and colour schemes. There was no other solution, but to cover them again. The prospect of driving around the course, and hiring aircraft at each destination to cover the aerial photography, struck me as a gross waste of time and money. It was better to hire a light aircraft and fly around the country, taking pictures as we went. The photographs in this book are the result. It was a great overview of a country in recession. To see how some parts of the country had adapted and even grown through it was amazing; to see how some parts had suffered was painful. Aviation is quick to adapt to new trends, as anticipation is an inherent part of the programmer's art; but retribution

is swift. Airlines who get it wrong are no longer with us, and the vacuum is quickly filled. It is the airport authorities who have to plan ahead in decades, and keep their heads with their multimillion pound projects, whilst the carriers come and go. The evidence in these pages affirms the confidence of British airport authorities in air transport as a growth industry. There is not a white elephant amongst them! In contrast, the only thing that moves in the docks today is water, and the ruin of the mines, the steelworks and heavy industry is apparent everywhere. Yet, aviation survives.

Statistically, it is the traditional airports that thrive.

Below:
Airwork Services Training School in the lush Perthshire countryside trains pilots and engineers for the world's airlines. They now have a Trident as an instructional airframe, in addition to the ex-Air Inter Viscount 700 which is hangared.

Britain is such a small country with such a good infrastructure that it is difficult for air transport to compete with ground services. (I remember contenders on the Manchester-London schedule being defeated by British Rail in the 1960s!) Yet, the mere fact that this is an island lends itself to air transport, and with the concept of the European Community and the perception that we are living in a shrinking world, aviation and the airports that support it are growing in global importance.

It is a fact that this book has become obsolete during its production. I found it impossible to move fast enough to keep up with developments in the industry. A Dan-Air skipper said once on landing at Manchester that this was the biggest building site in Britain which had its own airport! That work is now finished and Terminal 2 and its new domestic pier open. It is a model of an efficent international airport. Manchester's managers are now planning a second runway, which will move the airport on to a new plateau.

The other thing that struck me in our flight around the country was the number of farm strips that existed. I could pick my mother up in our Cessna 172 on a farm strip near her home in County Durham, and fly her back to Wycombe, a mere 30 minutes drive from my home in Ealing. With a microlight, there would be even more choice. But this does not detract from the growth of our major airports. May the politicians, and all the other prophets of doom please take note!

Capt. Austin J. Brown LBIPP.
Ealing 1993.

Above:
Jersey European regularly fly their Fokker F.27 500-Series Friendships on services to the Channel Islands and other European destinations alongside their newly-acquired BAe 146s and their faithful Short 360s.

Below:
Hughes 269C G-BATT pauses in the hover for the camera before taking off from the refuelling area at Blackpool.

ABERDEEN

Aberdeen is one of the country's busiest airports by virtue of its role in supporting the North Sea oil industry. As well as helicopter services provided by Bond, Bristow and British International Helicopters, scheduled and non-scheduled links are maintained with Europe in general and Scandinavia in particular. The airport is run by the BAA.

Above left:
Against a backdrop of deluging rain, a Bristow Helicopter's Tiger joins a Company S61N at the intersection of Runways 15 and 34 at Aberdeen, both en route to the rigs. This photograph gives some impression of the weather that the crews face on the North Sea operation.

Left:
Tug connected in preparation for push back, the British Airways Boeing 757 G-BMRE *Killyleagh Castle* awaits the return flight to London Heathrow.

Above:
A Cherokee Archer holds clear of Runway 34 as a Business Air Saab 340 rolls down a very wet surface on take-off for Dundee onward to Manchester.

Overleaf:
Bond Helicopters Super Puma G-PUMD taxies out from their helicopter terminal on the eastern apron, splashing its way though the puddles whilst the crew carry out their checks.

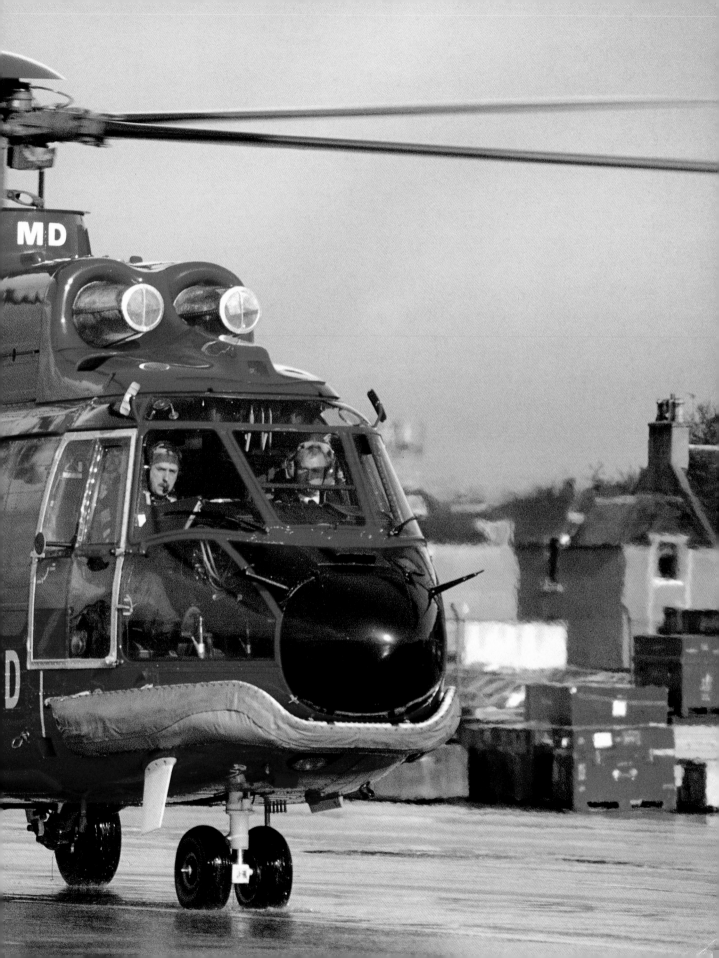

ALDERNEY

Above:
Operated by the States of Guernsey, the airport at
Alderney lies on a hill above the capital, St Annes,
and has approaches over rugged cliffs in both
directions. Aurigny Air Services operate Trislanders
on regular schedules and the Alderney Flying Club
offers flying training. What a delightful spot!

BELFAST (ALDERGROVE)

Below:
Dramatic nightime shot of the terminal at Belfast
from the the cockpit of a visiting airliner.

Overleaf:
Air Canada's 747-133, registration C-FTOC at
Belfast.

BIGGIN HILL

Biggin Hill, famed for its Battle of Britain connections, is now operated by Airports UK as a general aviation field for the London area. A delightful executive terminal has been built on the Western Apron and the installation of an ILS on Runway 21 has improved bad weather operations. The Southern apron is alive with numerous charter operators, maintenance organisations and flying clubs, and as part of the transfer from West Malling to Biggin Hill, Hunting Aircraft established a completions facility here for the Saab 340 in 1992.

Above:
The General Aviation Terminal from the west, showing the ample parking facilities and the threshold of Runway 21. As you can see, it's quite well subscribed.

Right:
The Navajo Chieftain G-POLO stands in front of Biggin's tower awaiting an emergency medical team to arrive and transfer a heart to the Royal Victoria Infirmary in Newcastle upon Tyne for a transplant operation.

Below:
Wearing the temporary Swedish registration SE-E03, Northwest Airlink's Saab 340B is rolled out of Hunting's hangar for the press on 11 May 1992, the 300th aircraft to be completed since the contract's commencement in 1982.

BIRMINGHAM INTERNATIONAL

Birmingham International's new terminal was opened in 1984, replacing the original building which was built in the mid 1930s. Then, in 1989, work began on a specially designed hub terminal in conjunction with British Airways. This is now open, and contributes to Birmingham's turnover of 3.8 million passengers per year.

Above:
The towbar is positioned on to the nose wheel of British Midland's Dash 7 G-BOAY during its turn round on the London Heathrow schedule. The clean lines of the functional, yet attractive new terminal, offer a graphic backdrop to the action.

Above left:
The old terminal building and control tower bear the marks of many modernisations in their 60 year history, but are still in use for Air Traffic Control, the Met Office, and a number of freight forwarding agencies. Here, a Brymon European BAe 1-11 G-BBME undergoes some engine maintenance.

Above:
The West Midlands Police Force's Twin Squirrel lifts off from the freight apron and heads north across Birmingham's new terminal.

Left:
Hooded by the shadow of the ground movements tower, one of Air 2000's Boeing 757s is refuelled prior to its departure for Cyprus on an inclusive tour charter.

Above & right:
Passengers disembark from one of Brymon European's Jetstream 31s at the new British Airways Eurohub. The company was formed in late 1992 by the amalgamation of Brymon Airways and Birmingham European, and flies the BAe 1-11, Dash 7 and Dash 8 in addition to the Jetstream 31.

BLACKPOOL

Above:
Blackpool Airport Fire and Rescue Services' newly
delivered Barracuda rescue vehicle stands on
readiness outside the fire station.

Above:
Bond's based Aerospatiale Dauphin 2 G-BKXE climbs out past Blackpool's distinctive tower en route to the rig operating in Morecambe Bay.

Right:
Passengers leave a Jersey European Short 360 which has just arrived from Belfast Harbour, whilst a Manx 360 awaits its passengers for the Isle of Man.

BOURNEMOUTH (HURN)

Bournemouth (Hurn) was opened for the RAF in 1941, but handed over to the Ministry of Civil Aviation in 1944. BOAC operated services from here until they transferred to Northolt and Heathrow in 1946. Vickers-Armstrongs then built a factory here producing the Varsity, the Viscount, and latterly, the BAC 1-11. Scheduled services have been operated through Bournemouth to the Channel Islands and France since the 1950s, and these have been joined by European inclusive tour operators, the latest being Palmair Flightline with their newly based BAe 146 Srs300. Flight Refuelling, the company founded by Sir Alan Cobham,(who pioneered air-to-air refuelling), is also based here, and flies target towing Falcon 20s under a contract with the Ministry of Defence for the Royal Navy. Channel Express, with their Heralds and Electras, are the largest based airline.

Above:
Dominating the foreground in this aerial view from the north-west is the old British Aerospace factory now owned by Lovaux (FLS).The passenger and cargo terminals are situated on the far side of the main 08/26 Runway, and the Needles and the Isle of Wight can just be seen in the background.

Above right:
Channel Express operate freight schedules from Bournemouth to the Channel Islands.One of their fleet of nine Heralds is seen parked in front of the terminal building, which was opened in 1984.

Right:
One of the five original Fieldmasters built by Desmond Norman stands in front of the Interair hangar. It was built as a crop spraying and fire fighting aircraft, and when photographed had just returned from a contract in France where it had worked as a water bomber.

BRISTOL LULSGATE

Above:
The terminal building at Bristol Airport has grown steadily over the years and has now been developed to the point where a new one, designed in the style of London Stansted, has been planned to replace it. The newest addition is the concrete apron on which the Air 2000 A320 is standing. Brymon European, whose Dash 8 is at the holding point of Runway 27, now have a permanent base and Aer Lingus use Bristol as a satellite hub. In fact, the airport is so successful that it contributes to the City Rate. The introduction of a loss leader, the offer of free car parking if you fly from Bristol Airport, has been so successful that the car parking area almost matches the apron area!

Above right:
The airport fire service is as efficient as their modern building looks!

Right :
KLM Cityhopper Fokker 50 noses towards the holding point of Runway 27, bound for Amsterdam.

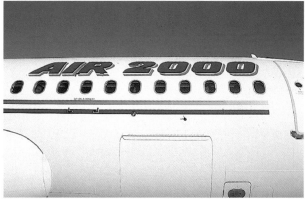

Above:
The morning rush is a mixture of charters and scheduled flights. I have watched inter-European schedules here grow in capacity from small commuter aircraft to jet airliners over the last 10 years, totally amazed that the catchment area could sustain it.

Left:
Cheyenne IV OE-FMM is representative of the many executive aircraft which visit Bristol on a regular basis. Behind is the South Western Electricity Board hangar, housing the company's Twin Squirrels which are used for inspection duties, and the Post Office's operations centre, which handles some 16 mail flights each night.

CAMBRIDGE

Above:
Previously based at Ipswich, Suckling Airways sole Dornier 228 lives at Cambridge and operates schedules to Amsterdam and Manchester. Cambridge's original art deco terminal building can be seen in the distance below the port wing; it is now used as airport offices by Marshalls of Cambridge who run the airport.

Above right:
From high above the centre line of Runway 05, Marshall's vast maintenance complex can be seen populated by Royal Air Force TriStars.

Right:
A near vertical view of the terminal shows a cross-section of light twins, the Suckling Dornier, a RAF Hercules C.3 and the Cambridge University Air Squadron Chipmunk and Bulldogs.

CARDIFF

Graphic view of the Brymon Dash 8 awaiting start-up whilst spectators look on from the balcony above.

Above:
And I thought that the terminal building at Cardiff was big! It is dwarfed by the new British Airways hangar designed to house three Boeing 747-400s at any one time.

Above right:
A catering vehicle draws away from an Inter European Airways Boeing 757 whilst passengers are chaperoned aboard a Brymon European Dash 8.

Right:
Cargo is unloaded from the Inter European Boeing 737-300 G-BNGM on the Eastern pier which is now equipped with air bridges.

CARLISLE

34

Left:
A Vulcan dominates the historic aircraft section at Carlisle as seen in this aerial view. A selection of light aircraft are the only currently active machines seen during this lull in business.

Above:
The air traffic control office at Carlisle may not have the scale of facilities of the major international terminals but still provides an efficient and safe service.

COVENTRY

Above:
A Channel Express Herald picked out starkly in the morning light, apparently supporting Coventry!

Above right:
Air Atlantique's passenger configured Dakota G-AMRA tucked away in a corner of the hangar area, enjoying the winter sun. Their fleet now consists of ten DC-3s, two DC-6s, three Cessna 310s, two 402s, a 404, two Islanders and a Navajo Chieftain.

Right:
Dollar Air Services Aztec E G-BFBB cross-lit against the company's reception. Dollar have a major base at Coventry, flying Bell Jet Rangers, Aerospatiale Lamas and Twin Squirrels.

Overleaf: Aerial shot of the Midland Air Museum by the threshold of Runway 17. How many different types can you recognise? Answers in Bob Ogden's *Aircraft Museums and Collections of the World*, Volume 2 (Pages 54-55)! Or pay them a visit. They'll be pleased to see you!

DUNDEE

Right:
Business Air's evening schedule coming in to land on Runway 28 with the Tay Bridge and Fife in the background. The Saab 340 then continues through from Aberdeen to Manchester, returning after dark.

Left:
Dundee Airport is built entirely on reclaimed land on the shores of the River Tay. As a grass strip in the late 1960s when I trained at Perth, it occupied the field to the east, but the obstacle clearance over the City and the Tay railway bridge in particular was insufficient for commercial operations, hence the new site. You can just pick out a Cessna 150 climbing out on left base having taken off on Runway 28.

Above:
Business Air's Saab taxies out in the failing light.

EAST MIDLANDS

Above:
Awaiting the night mail invasion at EMA, Post Office trucks are assembled into trains according to destination. The British Midland fleet relaxes in the background, along with a few other night-stopping aircraft.

Above right:
G-GNTA, the Saab 340 previously photographed at Dundee, stands surrounded by baggage trolleys, trucks and fuel tanker as they greet it simultaneously on its arrival. The company flies passengers by day, and contract mail by night, making the most of their capital investment.

Right:
On an adjacent stand, Aurigny's Short 360 receives the same treatment.

Above:
A girl in a wheelchair waves to me as she prepares
to board a Britannia Boeing 757 en route to the sun.

Right:
One of British Midlands short DC-9s, a Series 15,
photographed on short finals over the power station
from the visitor centre alongside the threshold of
Runway 27.

EDINBURGH

Below:
Almost ready for push back, this British Airways ATP G-BTPC is one of thirteen flying on the Highlands and Islands routes in Scotland.

Left:
Who's watching who? Ground operations are overseen by the ground movements controller, monitored obviously, in turn, by some higher authority. Or does it just identify the squawks?

Right:
A Loganair Jetstream 31 smiles for the camera, flanked by an Air UK BAe 146 and the BA ATP. The Jetstream 31s in the Loganair fleet have now been joined by a big brother, the 27 seat Series 41

EXETER

Left:
Wessex Air Charter's Piper Navajo Chieftain stands in the summer sunshine in front of Exeter's terminal building, overlooked by the spectators' balcony.

Overleaf top
A couple with young children pre-board a Spanair MD-83 en route to the Iberian peninsula.

Overleaf below:
A Turbo Commander gets locked up for the night under the watchful gaze of Exeter's modern control tower.

GLASGOW

Above:
Glasgow Airport slips into a sleepy lull following the evening rush on a winter's evening in 1992. The ATP is settling down for a night stop on the stand, but the 757 just visible behind it will be off to London within the hour.

Left:
The new passenger check-in hall is in fact an atrium built between the old and new terminals.

Above:
Unmistakably Glasgow, this newly arrived Northwest Airlines DC10 changes crews for the return flight across 'the Pond'. Not too many years ago such flights would have routed through Prestwick as a matter of course until there was a change in Government policy.

Above top:
This Cessna P.206 is the only float plane licensed in Britain to fly commercial charters from A to B. Based here at Glasgow, it is operated by Captain Bob Swainston of Aerofloat and expertly handled by ExecAir who run the General Aviation Terminal.

Above:
The British Airways ATP 'Papa Kilo' awaits its passengers at the domestic pier, off on another schedule around the Highlands.

Left:
Locked on to the ILS, this DC-9 descends through a blazing sunset towards the threshold of Runway 23.

GLOUCESTERSHIRE

Above:
Flight One's Twin Pioneer, highlighted by the low autumn sun while parked by the new control tower complex at Gloucestershire Airport.

Top right:
The Air Corbière Cessna Caravan II operates a schedule to and from Jersey. Air Corbière are the scheduled wing of Air Atlantique.

Right:
The sun breaks through the heavens over a Cessna 340A as evening clouds draw in.

GUERNSEY

Above:
Loganair's BAe 146-200 G-OLCA noses in to Stand 18 on a summer schedule from Glasgow.

Top right:
Built originally by Britten-Norman with island-hopping in mind, Aurigny's Trislanders are still going strong after all these years. They operate ten aircraft, including the famous JOEY plane, which spawned a delightful series of children's cartoon adventure books.

Right:
Aurigny's sole Short 360 flies passengers by day and freight by night. It is seen at East Midlands on a night mail service on Page 45.

HUMBERSIDE

Above:
The airport at Humberside hides its Bomber Command roots very well; it has been rebuilt in such a way that it looks like a new development. The long, low, modern terminal can be seen in the distance behind this visiting Super King Air.

Left:
One of the Queen's Flight's immaculate BAe 146 CC.2s ZE700 stands under escort on the apron, awaiting the return of its royal passengers.

Overleaf top:
An engineer stands by as his colleague spools up the engine of this Bond Helicopters Sikorsky S76A for a ground run prior to its departure to a nearby oil rig.

Overleaf below:
Newair operate a regular schedule into Humberside from Copenhagen with their Jetstreams. The cement factory and associated quarry in the background are a major landmark for inbound aircraft.

ISLE OF MAN

Above:
An aerial shot of Ronaldsway and Castletown,(on the left), whilst overflying to Belfast at 10,000ft. The classic star shape of the runways ensured that no runway could be more than 30 degrees out of wind. And the wind is quite strong, as can be seen by the "white horses" on the sea's surface.

Overleaf:
Caught under the halo of a double rainbow, this Datapost liveried Short 360 gleamed in the sun after its natural wash out on the tarmac at Ronaldsway, whilst everyone else sheltered from the rain. This photograph was taken before the terminal underwent extensive modernisation over the winter of 1992/93.

LAND'S END

Above:
The airfield at Land's End from the south, showing the three grass runways. Isles of Scilly Sky Bus operate five Pilatus Britten-Norman Islanders from Land's End on regular schedules to and from St Mary's in the Scilly Islands.

LEEDS / BRADFORD

Previous page:
A fine aerial shot of Leeds/Bradford's new terminal building on a day when Concorde was flying a specially arranged pleasure flight out over the Bay of Biscay to allow its passengers to experience a mixture of supersonic speed and luxury.

Above:
The terminal in profile as seen from the Yorkshire Light Aircraft Club on the south side of the airfield.

LIVERPOOL

Below:
A landing on Runway 09 neccessitates a long
approach over the River Mersey. Can you pick out
the Piper Cherokee just over the piano keys?

Above:
Liverpool's new terminal was built alongside the new runway on the north bank of the Mersey to the east of the old airport. It was not possible to develop the old site any further, and historic Speke Hall had to be protected. So in reality, a new airport was built beyond the original boundary. The two are still connected by a long taxiway.

Above right:
Beech C-12s of the US Army have been regular visitors from Coleman Barracks in Germany since the closure of nearby Burtonwood as an active airfield in the 1960s.

Right:
Night operations at Speke. This Heavylift Belfast had just brought a cargo of car components in from Germany for the Ford factory at Halewood, which is just down the road. The oil refineries on the south bank of the Mersey glitter in the darkness.

LONDON HEATHROW

Above:
A Thai International Boeing 747-3D7 lifts off from Runway 27R as an American Airlines Boeing 767-323ER taxies out from Terminal 3 to the holding point.

Right:
Looking across to the Cargo Terminal from the Central Area, a new British Airways Boeing 737-436 climbs out across the frame and into the warm winter sunset.

Top:
Although LOT Polish Airlines have also invested in Boeing 737-400s and 500s, they still operate the Tu154M into London, but for how much longer? Here SP-LCD leaves for Warsaw.

Above:
British Airways Boeing 747-136 G-AWNJ *Bassenthwaite Lake* is prepared for service at Terminal 4 in May 1989. Still in service, BA's 100 Series Boeing 747s are being steadily replaced by the new two-crew 400 Series, 25 of which have been delivered.

Left:
Relatively new carrier into London Heathrow is Air Hong Kong who fly their attractive Boeing 747-132 freighters in on schedules.

Overleaf:
Bird's eye view of Terminal 4 and Hunting's Executive Jet Centre taken from helicopter route H9 in 1992.

Above left:
South African Airways Boeing 747-244B ZS-SAM *Drakensberg* taxies into T3 past the new covered walkways which have been constructed to the north of Terminal One.

Left:
The American 767-323ER, photographed taxiing out earlier, climbs away into a clear blue winter sky. American Airlines connect to 203 US cities from London.

Above:
One of the many former Eastern Bloc operators to purchase Western equipment is Czechoslovakian Airlines who now fly the Boeing 737-500 into Heathrow.

Above:
ETOPS Boeing 767-322ER of United Airlines
precedes a company 747SP to the holding point of
Runway 09R in the summer of 1992.

Right:
British Midland DC-9 crew await clearance for push
back from the domestic pier of Terminal One at
Heathrow.

LONDON GATWICK

Above:
An impressive line-up of Jumbo tails greets you
when you walk up on to the balcony of the specta-
tors' terrace at Gatwick. Virgin, once restricted to
Gatwick, now have slots at Heathrow, and are
expanding even more with their latest order for the
Airbus A340. We all wait, with baited breath, for
Richard Branson's next move.

Above:
The People Mover makes its driverless way over to the South Terminal Satellite, whilst a 747 and two 767s await their passengers.

Above right:
The new North Terminal can be seen behind the South Terminal Satellite which is hosting, amongst other aircraft, the Nationair Boeing 747-1D1 C-FFUN. This aircraft had been a regular visitor for many, many years with its previous owner, Wardair of Canada.

Right:
City Flyer Express ATR42 threading its way to its stand past the ex-Dan Air Boeing 737-400s which had just been taken over by British Airways.

Top:
DAS Air Cargo operate this Boeing 707-338C as a freighter out of Gatwick regularly.It is seen here just unsticking off Runway 26L.

Above:
The inclusive tour sector is represented here by this Airtours McDonnell Douglas MD-83 taking off for warmer climes. Against market trends, Airtours have expanded during the recession, and have filled some of the vacuum left by the demise of operators such as Air Europe. The company is based at Manchester and operates eight MD-83s.

Right:
A British Airways Boeing 737-408 pulls out of the cul de sac en route to the holding point. The back-drop is of the original Gatwick terminal prior to its expansion.

Left:
Another newcomer to the market place recently is Excalibur Airways. Their strong company logo on the tail fin of this A320-212 gives colour and perspective to this alternative view of the New North Terminal.

Above:
Strong back lighting throws a shadow of the Pratt & Whitney PW120 engine over the forward fuselage of this City Flyer Express ATR42 taxiing in after a flight from Newcastle. City Flyer were the first company in the UK to put the ATR42 on the British register.

LONDON STANSTED

Above:
Richard Rogers' expansive terminal building at Stansted Airport is a landmark in British architectural design as well as being functional. At the moment, it has an air of desertion, but the infrastructure is in place for the expansion that will inevitably come to London's third airport.

Right:
Detail of the columns supporting the canopy at the front of the building.

Above:
Passenger's eye view of the entrance into the terminal from the rail terminal which connects London (Liverpool Street) with the airport at 30 minute intervals. The unique design of the skylights provides the interior of the building with a subtle diffused light, reminiscent of being inside a white tent.

Above:
Heavylift Cargo Airlines operate six Antonov An124 Ruslans in conjunction with the Russian company Volga Dnepr. The first to be seen was CCCP-82042, which is photographed here at Heavylift's Stansted base.

LONDON CITY

Above:
The unique Docklands site of the London City airport.

Overleaf:
Brymon Airways Dash 7 parked at London City Airport,which is sited in Docklands between the Royal Albert Dock and the King George V Dock. Designated a STOLport, it has recently allowed the first jets, the quiet STOL BAe 146, to operate.

LUTON

Above:
Neon Tiger adorns the entrance to the Luton Flying
Club, who have been operating since 1938.

Above:
The Ryanair BAe 1-11 531FS EI-CCU roars off Luton's easterly runway on its way back to Dublin on the lunchtime schedule. Ryanair operate a mixture of British Aerospace and RomBac (Romanian built) 1-11s, as well as three ATR42s.

Above right:
Air Foyle operate this TNT BAe 146-200 Quiet Trader on night parcel delivery flights alongside six other 200 and 300 Series models.

Right:
Graphic view of the passenger arrivals entrance from beneath the wing of the Monarch Airlines Boeing 737-33a G-MONV. Note the oval shape of the cowling of the Boeing's CFM56 engine, designed to increase its ground clearance.
Courtesy London Luton Airport PRO

97

Above:
Luton is a popular destination for visiting executive jets. This view from the now disused Ground Movements Tower captures a Gulfstream IV and a Falcon 50 on the apron, whilst one of Britannia Airways Boeing 767s is being towed away from the stand. Two Boeing 757s of the Spanish company LTE stand outside the Monarch hangar. *Courtesy London Luton Airport PRO/Studio Neill*

LYDD

Above:
Wheeling left in a steep turn over Lydd's terminal, Richard Goode puts us on to the dead side for landing on Runway 22 in his Extra 300. Lydd is a convenient point for launching off in your light aircraft cross-Channel and Love Air operate a regular schedule to Le Touquet using a Navajo Chieftain.

Right:
About to cross the threshold of 04 into the downwind
position for the landing on 22, we get a good overview of the field, showing its proximity to the coast
and the sandy barrenness of this corner of Kent.

Below:
From ab initio to commercial jet! This photograph of
a line-up of Piper Tomahawks of the South East
College of Air Training leading in to a privately
registered Boeing 727 typifies many a young man's
dream.

MANCHESTER

Above:
Passenger's view of Manchester Airport's terminals
from Runway 24 just after take-off. The new
Terminal 2 and its associated apron is on the left.

Above top:
An American Airlines Boeing 767 leaving Runway 24 *en route* back to the USA.

Above:
An Emirates A310 rotates on Runway 24 behind Manchester School of Flying's Piper Cherokee 140 parked on the southside. A recently arrived Air Hong Kong 747 freighter unloads in the distance.

Left:
The newly opened Terminal 2 has some 14 air-bridges and shows an impressive line-up of visiting airliners.

Above:
Aerial view into the sun from the north following heavy rain shows the immense size of Terminal 2 and its apron.

Above right:
An Air Columbus Boeing 727 taxies out for take-off from Terminal A on a charter flight back to Portugal.

Right:
Air Kilroe's Super Jetstream 31, complete with underbelly speedpak, stands outside their general aviation terminal near the main terminal building. The company fly three Jetstreams, two Super King Airs, a Navajo Chieftain and a Partenavia P68B on passenger and freight charters, air ambulance and aerial photography flights.

MANSTON

Above:
Manston is operated on a joint civil/military basis. Here an RAF controller talks an aircraft down on the Precision Approach Radar (PAR) which can bring the aircraft down to wheels touching even in zero visibility in an emergency.

Right:
This low aerial shot gives some impression of the width of Manston's runway: it is four times the width of a normal runway and used to have the added facility of being able to be covered with a foam carpet in the event of an emergency landing by an aircraft with a disabled undercarriage. This facility has now been withdrawn. To give some sense of scale, those aircraft parked on the dispersals are Boeing 707s.

Left:
Demonstrating the increasing competitiveness of Russian operators, this Il-76T newly registered with the RA prefix was taking on steel girders for a flight to Cameroon. It was previously a testbed aircraft, but is now operated by Elfair on commercial services.

NEWCASTLE

Above:
This aerial view from high over the extended centre line of Runway 07 shows the modern terminal with its recent rail connection with the Newcastle Metro system. The maintenance area and the flying club are on the apron to the south of the runway. The Newcastle VOR/DME is positioned to the north of the parallel taxyway just west of the new fire station.

Right:
The covered walkway leading from the Metro station to Newcastle's impressive terminal building.

Opposite:
A jumbo sized shadow intercepts this British Airways Boeing 737-236 as it approaches the flare on to Runway 25 in the Winter light, inbound from London Heathrow.

Left:
Sticking its nose out of the hangar on a rainy afternoon in October 1992, one of Gill Air's Short 330s obviously felt unmoved by the weather, and stayed put.

Below:
One of the ex Aer Lingus Short 360s acquired by Gill Aviation who are based at the airport. They now operate a total of ten 330/360s on schedules and night mail services.

NORWICH

Above:
High angle over the top of Norwich's terminal shows the new terminal building settled amongst the original hangars and buildings of what was at one time RAF Horsham St Faith.In addition to the aircraft parked on the tarmac, you can just pick out a Spitfire parked behind the Airport Hotel in the bottom left hand corner of the photograph.

Above right:
Titan Airways base a Short 330 here for use on their Post Office night mail service. Norwich is Air UK's main maintenance facility.

Right:
Directflight now operate six Cessna Caravan IIs out of Norwich and Prestwick. The Caravan II is not to be confused with the Caravan I. It is basically a Cessna Titan with turboprops, and is only made by the French division of Cessna Aircraft based at Reims.

PERTH

Above:
Airwork Services Training School in the lush
Perthshire countryside trains pilots and engineers
for the world's airlines. This view over the apron
shows the Piper Cherokees and Cessna 150s used
for abinitio pilot training, with Instrument Rating
training being carried out on Cessna 310s.

PLYMOUTH

Above:
This aerial photograph was taken shortly after the opening of the new second runway (13/31), which is some 350 metres longer than the original 06/24.

Right:
Bar boxes are loaded on to the Brymon Dash 7 G-BRYD prior to its departure for Heathrow on a grey day in October 92. The modern terminal building complex with control tower and fire station can be seen in the background.

PRESTWICK

Left:
The Canadian Armed Forces have been regular visitors to Prestwick for years, transiting through to and from their bases in Germany. Here the tail of a Lockheed C130E Hercules frames the Ground Movements Control Tower at the end of the international pier.

Above:
Airbrake unlocked, a TNT BAe 146-200 stands idle in the evening light ready to fly on the parcel contract that night. In the distance, the familiar profile of the British Aerospace factory which builds the Jetstream 31 and 41s.

Above:
Looking inland from the Ayrshire coast, Prestwick's 2,987m main runway creates an impressive sight. To the left is the British Aerospace complex, with its factory and the College of Air Training, and beyond that, HMS *Gannet,* the Royal Navy base that flies the 819 Squadron Sea Kings on search and rescue missions.

SCILLY ISLES

Above:
A visiting Cessna 337D Super Skymaster parked in front of the modest but well designed terminal at St Mary's in the Scilly Isles.

SHOREHAM

Above:
The 1930s Art Deco terminal building is a delight. Our steed for the round Britain trip, which Dick Flute and I flew in October 1992, is parked conveniently in front of it for this photograph. A Reims Cessna F172N of the Wycombe Air Centre at Booker, it never let us down though we flew it sometimes in the most appalling conditions.*

*Read about this once-in-a-lifetime trip in *Cessna 172 Round Britain* in Ian Allan's 'From the Flight Deck' series. Published August 1993.

Right:
The neat little airfield at Shoreham is situated on the west bank of the River Adur less than a mile inland from the south coast. It is the headquarters of the Popular Flying Association, and is a very busy and friendly little field. It has one hard runway (03/21) and two grass runways.

SOUTHEND

Left:
Night departure of the Air Malta inclusive tour schedule, illuminated by the lights of the terminal. October 1992.

Above:
The British Air Ferries Viscount 808C G-BBDK is one of eleven operated by the company, in addition to a Herald, a Friendship, four BAe 1-11s and a BAe 146.

Right:
This view of Southend demonstrates well the number of maintenance and storage facilities to be found on the airfield, as well as flying clubs, airlines and general aviation operators. British Air Ferries are by far the largest operators, with Heavylift Cargo Airlines Maintenance Unit coming a close second.

SOUTHAMPTON

Above:
Extensive development of the apron area is under way at Southampton's Eastleigh Airport in this aerial view taken in October 1992.

Right:
Passengers head for the arrivals hall inbound from the Channel Islands on an Air UK Friendship, whilst a Jersey European F-27 is turned around on the adjacent stand.

SUMBURGH

Above:
Sumburgh derives much of its traffic from the oil industry as this collection of visiting Swedish and Norwegian business types suggests. In the background helicopters on oil rig work also stand ready.

Left:
A Loganair ATP in the last few feet before touchdown on Sumburgh's Runway 15.

TEESSIDE

Right:
Passengers trickle aboard a British Midland DC-9
bound for London Heathrow on the evening service.

Below:
A Belgian registered white-tailed Boeing 757 stands
against a sunset of lenticular clouds on the western
apron at Teesside. Its registration is OO-TBI and it
is leased by to Trinity Aviation Limited.

Bottom:
Evening reflections are mirrored in the starboard
fuselage in this detail of the 757.

Above:
An aerial view of the former RAF station known as
Middleton St George looking east towards Teesport
and the Teesside Industrial area. It has a well developed terminal area, and the runway's extension to
2,291m can be clearly seen.